Early Poems

Early Poems 1966-1969

Jonas Zdanys

Copyright © 2020 by Jonas Zdanys.
All rights reserved.

ISBN 978-1-7338882-2-6
Manufactured in the United States of America

Black Spruce Press
blacksprucepress.org
blacksprucepress@gmail.com
Design by forgetgutenberg.com

Contents

How It Happened / 1
Incidental Consequences of a Barren Life / 3
In a Time of War / 4
The End of the War / 5
Miracle / 6
The Final Admission of the Pain of Fall / 7
Midnight / 8
Light / 9
Arrival / 10
Dusk / 11
Spring at Narragansett / 12
Postcard from New Haven / 13
Point Judith / 14
On Thomas Hart Benton's Murals... / 15
"Mount your friends..." / 17
Self Portait, June 24th / 19
2 Poems / 20
Bridegroom's Monologue / 21
Blue Trail / 22
A Trip Upon a Magic Swirling Ship / 23
1968 / 28
my balls are gone / 29
A Children's Story / 30
Three / 31
Sister Josepha / 33
The Fisherman / 34
Thoughts in a Rainy Season / 35
Rocky Hill Avenue, Autumn 1955 / 36
Sunday 1955 / 38
The Cold Wind / 39
Trees / 40
Terminal Days / 41
Soliloquy: November Eighteenth / 42

The Garage / 44
McVey's Barn / 46
Her Drawing / 47
Yellow / 48
Listen / 50
an exercise in rhyme / 51
daisies, lilacs, violets, and dandelions / 52
Thoughts in a Dry Season / 54
Birdsong / 56
A Very Good Day / 57
Golgotha / 58
August 20th / 59
Through the Looking-Glass / 60

This small book is a pocket companion to my retrospective *Collected Poems 1970–2020*. It presents poems I wrote between 1966 and 1969, as a teenager. A few of these were published in high school literary magazines during those years but otherwise have not appeared before in print. These earliest poems come from an old and well-worn orange folder marked "Collected Poems 1966–1969" that tumbled from drawer to drawer in various houses for more than fifty years. That handwritten title scrawled across that cover brings a smile to my face now, the boy playing the man, finding significance fifty years ago in the compilations of those three early years of writing. I suppose I saved that folder all this time because, at some level, I have been thinking about making these earliest poems more public in some way. I do so now because my *Collected Poems* has been published and these early pieces seem to me to mark the beginning of several continuing thematic commitments and explorations that have found differing voices, structures, and expressions over the years in my work.

I have been tempted to rewrite some of these poems but have not done that, except for one or two small edits here and there. There were a few that seemed particularly in need of fixing, but I didn't want to impose the perspectives of the half century that has passed since I wrote these on the exuberances and quick emotions of a teenager, so I left them as they first found their places in that orange folder. The poems in this collection are presented in reverse order, beginning with some poems written when I was a freshman in college and ending with poems I wrote when I was sixteen. I can hear that voice as I read these poems and remember how serious that boy was. I remember as well that I was always trying to "do it right" as a beginning poet. I had a great deal to learn, of course, and the awkwardness of some of the writing in this presentation is part of that early dedication, part of a foundational stage, in shaping that move toward successful writing. I continue to do my best to learn. And though my work now may be different from the pieces I was writing fifty years ago, I'm happy to claim the poems in these pages as my own.

JZ

How it Happened

Last night God stretched his hand
through the open bedroom window
and gently touched my face.
I woke, suddenly cold,
and thinking a strong wind
was blowing outside,
closed and locked the window.
The hand dug into the cooling ashes,
scattered them beyond the fence.
Dead-white spots mottled the ivy.

*

He stops and remembers something.
The smells of spilled whiskey
thicken in the room.
He thinks:
I will always be
a weary engraver of silence.
He starts to mourn.
Eternity sprouts uncovered and blind
beneath his feet, creeps
with the things under the earth
until the last sound dies away.
He falls into the world.
The world falls into him.

*

Unconditional surrender
is our one gift to the world.
That's what they taught us.
I can't remember anything else.
I stand in the wind
like a tree without roots
trying to catch myself

from spinning off the earth,
grasping every passing stain of time,
every patch of light.

*

I don't know how I knew this.
I called out from a distance.
Each face in the heavens,
each name underfoot.
No one can separate
your beginning and my end.
You follow without moving,
midway to the rooftop,
murmuring every name
that rusts in your mouth.

*

Hiding behind the curtains
I saw the mosaic of my life
broken to pieces
by old women dressed in rags

I sleep in torn curtains
my shadow hides on the mosaic floor
my wings heave
with the flutterings of burned rags

(1969)

Incidental Consequences of a Barren Life

1.
A childless woman,
barren,
wanting to nurse children,
drowned herself.
We found her body
washed up by the lake,
breasts crusted with leeches.

2.
She rises from the water.
Eyes clouded white.
Unable to see,
wound with nets of grass,
she searches hopelessly
for her unborn children.

3.
Stopping by the water she asks:
Who will anoint us, the melancholy dead?
The water tried but could not manage.
Sand drinks in blood,
desire, and the darkness of day.
The dark stream trickles away,
air grows thick, clouds vanish.

(1969)

In a Time of War

1.
The raven's wing poked
God's blind eye.
The eye began to tear.
The world began to bleed.

2.
Rifles dreamed of soldier's fingers
and unexpectedly shot themselves.
In the morgue corpses died like fallen angels.

3.
The sun burned out and everything froze.
Soldiers' eyes and lips turned black.
The moon laughed.

4.
Dolls in the shop windows
trembled and wept
when an army of unwound clocks
unceremoniously passed by.

5.
We met the last soldiers.
Their pants were torn,
hair and faces spattered with dried blood.
There's no way out, they said,
there's no end.
The night was cold,
the moon black in the red sky.

(1969)

The End of the War

restlessness and resignation

the paddle-wheel turns
across a string of sky
on the thin horizon

astonishing and beautiful
gritty with the distortion
of a lost love, our lost love

it gives me no courage
no hope for a cleaner narrative
the literal unlikely

at midnight my bones hurt
I avoid everyone in the hall
feel only the shrapnel of

restlessness and resignation

(1969)

Miracle

They said it was a miracle,
but we understood what it truly was:
the black light of stars
bound together words and wounds
with magic and madness
and traced the final question
on the red tiles of the floor.
It has no unassailable answer.

(1969)

The Final Admission of the Pain of Fall

dead
branches
against
the sky
whiter
than
bones
leavings
of birds
returning
home
to
die
one
for
the
other
and
October's
colors
when
night
darkens
irritate
my
eyes
this
is
enough
for
now

(1969)

Midnight

The clock strikes
on a web of air

The moon shines low
in the meadow

and leaves fall easily
in gardens as the wind stills

Listen
do not speak
listen

The clock strikes
on a web of air

(1969)

Light

Light is the watchman
of the world's edge

it sings the secret rhymes
of childhood

teases us across valley
crammed with deadfalls

holds us as we jab
our roots at heaven

(1969)

Arrival

What birds died
in this sand,
starfish
stiffened in the sun?

Shells in piles by the tideline,
gulls and seaweed
breaking
on black waves.

We climb across
wet rocks, don't know
how we got here
or why.

(1969)

Dusk

The light will set soon
there
along the shore
where the winds cross

there
on the old waters
where birds fly
after sharp notes
black mouths locked open

there
where fog breaks
out of darkness
where buoys ring
and waves stiffen with night

Stop wait
I have had enough

Everything will end this way

Sunset on your face
the sea blue and yellow
in the distance
the harbor's hard dunes
abandoned and red

(1969)

Spring at Narragansett

Clocks stop ticking
in mudflat Narragansett
when summer residents
—the prop plane set—
fly to winter wonderland tenements
in Waukegan and Chickering.

The "finest-grain-sand"
plush private beach
is now dotted
with washed up bottles of clorox bleach
and building planks, sea-soaked and rotted,
the signposts of the new promised land.

Food for flies, a seaweed clump hung
on a storm dyke rots in the sun.
Occasional footprints of dogs,
unleashed, on the run,
lead to urine-stained driftwood logs.
Waves lap the shore like a dark dog's tongue.

A dying horseshoe crab in torment,
the only life at Narragansett now,
crawls on the beach,
pushing sand before it like a broken plow
toward water it cannot reach.
The sea casts up its excrement.

(1969)

Postcard from New Haven

L,
I agree that
we had to leave each other
because you wanted
the loose happiness of dogs
and children
and I dreamed again
last night
that I was lost
and damned
with words,
weaving dreams
in an endless chain
the jangles the world.
I think there was some sense
of triumph in that,
a path between two rows,
that we do not have to interpret,
which isn't hard to understand.
I raise my glass
to you and your new lover
in celebration
of an unclaimed fate.
Sincerely,
J

(1969)

Point Judith

I wrote your name
in the sand
and watched the waves
wash it away

as gulls on the wharfpiles
and piers,
open-eyed, dived
for bluefish.

Now the night
above my head
is frozen to clouds
and stars.

The wave that took
your name beckons
the bird that crosses
the track of the moon.

(1969)

*On Thomas Hart Benton's Murals in the
New Britain Museum of American Art*

get next to god
flashes the bluewhite neon sign
get next to god
while prim proper people
dance and pitch horseshoes
in the shadow of the steeple
gray smoke rising blues
the bricked chimney line
makes the blue windows bleaker

a partyhatted playboy
and a brassy blonde toy
with burlesque love
in the choir
loft beneath the drumming
wings of a dove
tongues of fire
telling of the second coming

get next to god
flashes the bluewhite neon sign
get next to god
sings the gold and silver
plated saxophone choir
while overhead a faceless
potbellied angel on a wire
announces that all is his
all is theirs and none is mine
  *

a balding farmer
sits wearily
on his wagon
holding his work-worn face

in gnarled hands
and yawns deep and long
as two bony-rumped
knock-kneed white mules
strain to pull
the grain-laden buckboard
up the mud-stained hill
as a jeering long-legged
unshaven tramp
lies under an overripe
apple tree
snoring snoring
head back head back snoring

(1968)

"Mount your friends," He said, "when they don't mount you."

the sermon on mounting's dun
he'll roam through black of day
sad light of day
when curve unbends
to shoreless run
out past the time away
that never ends

let's go
let go
lesson:
lessen
your neighbor
not his burden

proof of god
that never awed
nothing higher
than your desire

sing unwaivering songs:
bad day body faints
suffering all its wrongs
head thorned with cold restraints
while the crossed fool longs
to rescue sinners and saints

he crossed me up
after the last sup
where whine
was poorred brine

mary mary
quite contrary
did his wood harden
in your garden

ring around the rosary
pocket full of nails
pulling cloaks and underwear
out from wooden pails

hot cross
buns
hot cross
buns
hot cross
buns

(Easter 1968)

Self Portrait, June 24th

A shining wreathed reflection
in the painted window,
wood burnished to the grain.
My face and the walls
the color of clay, this mistake
my present form, numb
on the opposite side
of the shortest days of winter.
The world doubles.
I sit trapped in the dark
like the one who poured out
the holy river's waters
and danced in the long shadow
of the future, foreshadowing
something, somewhere
I could not climb.
The year gutters out uninvited.
The light does not grow brighter.
The three trees on the hill
root themselves in the breech,
the pitch of the sky oblique.
I see him through shut eyes.
I feel his last confession.
I hear how our
heavy heads sing mutely
together in the ashes
of this gathering night
dance, Salome, dance

(1968)

2 poems

flowers

leaves
and
grass

a
girl
dancing

at
mid-
night

alone

*

muddy
boards
by
the
barn
a
thrush
singing

(1968)

Bridegroom's Monologue

We're one.
We lie in a room
filled with sun.
Chain smoking

until noon
I weighed the past
and the future
coming fast.

Lying here
no longer alone
I fear
what time will bring.

My t-shirted back
is covered
with deep black
stains;

sweat has matted
my hair;
cigarette smoke
stales the air;

covers hide
the cringing
man inside
the sagging bed.

I lift my hand,
now cold now hot;
our fingers meet
and knot.

(1968)

Blue Trail

We came to Blue Trail.
There were traces
of other visitors:
horses and hikers
had left their refuse,
scattered ashes
and burned sticks
marred the green-ringed
gray rocks,
gave the woods
a used look.
The reservoir looked small
from where we sat
on the stone ledge.
Trees hid us
from the road below.
We fell asleep in the
pale light, locked together
here in the currents of trees
and water and dreams,
waking surprised when
it was too dark to see.

Leaving,
I walked by
our hidden bicycles.

(1968)

A Trip Upon a Magic Swirling Ship

I

    a multiunconscious
    consciousness
    lurching
    in the darkness of the air
    of the future
    whimpering disarmed enigma
    kaleidoscopically dense & lost
    red leggings of sawdusted silk
    clutching calliope
    cardboard & ticky-tack
    flying through
    unreal realness deep
    memories catalogued
    in the twilight zone
    of the ear
    & eye
    & taste
    & smell
    & hard rub
    of soundless unsounds hollow
    brave new worlds
    disordered & brooding
    in the labyrinth of indifference
    bleeding in all affairs
    of the bodymind of life
    mountains valleys flowers flame
    ice bones
    stiff & stumbling whispers
    of black stars
    after the hunt frightened & treed
    reeling & falling up the stairs
    blindeyedcockinhand
    I cry to the winding wind

hear my plea
but the unwinding winding wind
not prone to any mechanical death
the thing itself heads or tails
clenched fists pounding
the immortal roads
unheard my plea
as it swung like a broken bell
& pierced the blind vortex
of death&life
sullen stacks of gook bodies
yellow against the blue sky like a scar
on America's face
glass breaking when thrown against
the green wall
thevietcongarealwayswrong
myfellowamericans
myfellowamericans
who goes all the way with LBJ
trickydick
negro soldiers no longer speechless
in the tricked attack
fuckyoufuckyoufuckyoufuckyou
motherfucker
honkydon'tlearnhegonnaburn
if America don't come 'round
we got to burn it down
you better get some guns brother
the only thing the honky respects
is a gun
dark will not lighten
light will not darken
a dog with one cropped ear slides by
impaled disaster
a black angel
on a pitchblack monday afternoon
at seven o'clock

under the black highway bridge
crowed the inarticulate master
    & all life
    & all death
    & all life
hear my plea
    & all people
    of life & death
hear my plea
hear my plea
hear my plea
O Lost in the Piercing Glare
O Cut in the Ragged Pump
O Fucked in the Manic Palm
O West Wind of Sallow Endings
& Shadows & dead telephones
lurching along the road
mandala lysergic acid pot
you are   useless now
a hollow crown
a cold belly
crossed legs
conducted love against my will
in the wicked lodge
images of what is possible
on satiated sundays
live said the god made man
through him in him with him
man is godisman is god
welcome to the valley of mind
naked paradise of despair
loosed across the rim of the world
uncheering sideline sitters
rivers & unseenunhearduntouched
demons & the dominion
of brown pocks & liverslop
radio is good god

sage of earthly pleasures
random bad fathers
in line for the epitaph
crucified songs carpenters
from galilee
hung up hands twitching ageless
deathlike
in a vague room of the universe
pull yourself together turn to flame
in the rain
fight against the war the war the war
the indistinct huts on the horizon
burning
shout
piss
weep
for the fractured the violent work
on the lost field & the yellow man
though no one listens to me or you
stripped of identity
in the circus of the mad mind
not once but once&for all
in the bluegraysteely sky
the lostness of awakeness
the dangerousness of the hour
the inadequateness
of the hurrying pail
the splintered egg of life
the vermilion brush of blood
on forsaken existence
the last word
the final cut
& I cried when you cried
not once not twice but for you
eternally
the post man
the pot man

the captain of the sunken boat
your dead father
secretly when I stood back
away from the rest
your brothers & sister & mother
& so few others
when you buried him
in some soldiers' field
in a public grave in a rocky hill
you holding your face in your hands
weeping to yourself
shoulders shaking
standing alongside
the cold brown box
suspended above the dug dark hole
& the dead weeds singing
& constantly repeated
over lost connections
of understanding
strange changes two crooked roses
flowers picked from the seafloor
by drowned sailors
the empty mansion
of the perishing sun
strive in the night time spread
of unawareness
of unconsciousness
of discontented carnival
come come come
as I move with you
in you on you by you
come o come ah god! ah god!
I need you I need you I need you

I

(1968)

1968

from high above
the chalk-dry steeple
of the rock-brown
church petrified
crows tumble down
prophets
of the blind side
of love
blotting out
daylight
with their black
bodies
covering the hard
ticky-tack
street
kicking
their feet
in the air

everywhere
cardboard people
in the shadow
of the steeple
turn their white
blind eyes
from the sky
and tramp
round and round
pushing open beaks
into hard ground

(1968)

my balls are gone
perhaps for the last time
this time
the walls are closing in
grasping pulling
with invisible tendrils
my balls are gone
perhaps for the last time
this time
the walls are closing in

(1968)

A Children's Story

cold
we picked flowers
on the seafloor
& laughed
as we came up
for air
& found gold
& silver-
plated sea
gulls in lifeguard
chairs
blowing whistles
to come to shore
but blinded
breathless by that alone
we sank beneath the waves
again safe to search
no more

(1968)

Three

We walked under a row
of willow trees,
the girl with the
bright-streaked hair
and I, her pleated skirt
above her knees,
busy with love.
I touched her waist
as if to guide her
and she moved
my hand away,
the time given
as she turned instead
to kiss my mouth,
our footsteps,
hers and mine,
moving together again
as she closed her eyes
and opened her mouth
and her head
leaned back.

*

Her taut athletic body
pressed against me,
freckled nose
and soft wide mouth
touched my face.
She smiled.
Life was tennis
every Saturday afternoon,
a stop at the curio shop
after school.
She was the first girl

whose breasts I touched
and I told her
I was sorry as I kissed her,
my hand pressed
hard against her,
and she kissed me back.
One day that summer
things got changed around,
I stopped wanting
to see her. They told me
she pressed her hands
against her breasts
and called my name,
tried as she could
to cry me back.

*

Pixie-like,
short dark hair barely
covering her ears,
she laughed.
Her soft brown eyes
were fawn-like,
lips tender and insistent,
her hand reaching for me
and moving up and down,
up and down.
That's how the body does it.
Up and down.
It was a cool spring.
It rained all summer.

(1968)

Sister Josepha

Genuflecting, she blessed herself.
Her veil, covering virgin hair,
Pressed deeply into her aging forehead.
Rimless glasses bulged her dark eyes.
Her black habit was covered with dust.
Withered lips fervently and silently moved.
Arthritic hands were folded in prayer.
Rising, she stumbled, caught herself
On the altar, continued washing the floors.
I lit a candle by the statue of the Virgin Mother,
listened to Sister Josepha
as she raged at her Father.

(1967)

The Fisherman

The fisherman rises slowly,
Runs stiff fingers
Through his sparse hair,
Dresses again in brackish clothes.
He rigs the sails and with
Calloused hands stretches
His frayed nets
On thin gray sand.
He wipes his face
With his shirt sleeve,
Sees the figures of others
On the far shore, dressed in white,
Birds circling in and out along the wake,
Black banners waving forever
On a dark horizon.

(1967)

Thoughts in a Rainy Season

The great maple, one of the three
In our yard, rubbing its broad leaves
Against the slowly rusting storm windows,
Nobly fights the ungentle rain.

It was raining when I saw you
As I crossed the puddle-stained street.
You smiled and waved
As I ran to meet you, your lovely face
Quelled by my melancholy.
Your hand pressed mine in a warm caress.
Talk was confusion, a flurry
Of polite meaningless words.
I wanted you to stay but in a moment
You were gone – to the post office
Of all the garish places in our town.
Only the memory of your soft steps
As you turned and walked away remains.

The rain, a drizzle now, seems as distant
As our chance meeting.
The maple, swaying in the cold
Unseasonable breeze,
Is dark and austere against the dying sky.
Branches scratch the clouded glass
In a futile attempt to get in.

(1967)

Rocky Hill Avenue, Autumn 1955

The gray-black stone pile
by the gravel driveway stands
like an altar as we approach.
The air is brisk.

The fading-red garage,
splintered doors hanging beneath
a low-pitched roof, is empty
except for my discarded tricycle
and scattered unread newspapers.
It is a dark foreboding place.
We dare not enter.

We are dressed in autumn play clothes.
My thick insulated stone-gray outfit
makes me feel like an overstuffed scarecrow.
My brother, a toddler, a roly-poly red elf.

We hold each other's hands as we explore
the far corners of the fenced yard.
Gravel and hardening soil crunch beneath our feet
as we walk toward the magic rock pile.
We laugh.

Suddenly a dull black snake appears
on the pile and slithers toward us
calling me to stay in a hissing high-pitched voice.

I yell *Run!* not heeding the pleading
cries of the leaden snake.
Run! Run! Run!...

Thinking back to my brother's red cheeks
puffing with a child's exhaustion

as we ran for the safety of our house,
and how strangely amusing his awkward
movements appeared, I can't help now but laugh.

Yet,
I feel a strange longing to disappear
within those tortuous rocks,
safe from prying eyes,
safe in a hollow world
made of light brown cardboard ticky-tack.

Lost!

All I can do is run...

(1967)

Sunday 1955

people at the door
breaking free
from my mother's hand
I ran to the pantry
lined with pots and pans
and marks in the dust
on the floor
ran to the pantry
fast as I can
my heart will bust
and hid behind the curtain
drawn across the door
I would not move
locked in the pantry's
cut and groove
waiting for them to be gone
and done
cousins aunts and un-
cles voices calling me
straight to the core
baby baby
come out baby
be a man
if you can
they would not leave me
no matter what I did
there beneath the dust I hid
uncle in the morgue dying
later mother picked me
from the floor
clutching a pot and crying

(1967)

The Cold Wind

The sounds of Sunday afternoon
football followed us as we walked
through the leaf-spattered park.
Bare almost lifeless trees
swayed in the brisk breeze
scattering decaying yellow-orange leaves,
covering the dying flower beds.
Your hand pressed mine
in a warm caress.
We laughed.

It's snowing now.
Sunday is gone.
The window fogs
from the heat
of my pressed face.

A bell in the distance
begins to ring.
My weeping does not turn back
the cold wind.

(1967)

Trees

Only shadows now stand
Where trees once stood
Braving the winds
That shook the house
And rattled the old wooden
Storm windows.

The trees outside the bedroom wall
Stand like empty coat racks
In abandoned halls gathering dust.
Just yesterday
They hid this window
From the street.

Now their branches are bare,
Squeak against the dark
Window panes,
While above, in the clear
Night air, re-echo words
I once said to you.

(1967)

Terminal Days

The old gray maple
by the wooden fence
that surrounds the house
is decaying.
Rain taps against old rotting
wooden storm windows.
Inside, my grandfather is dying.
Young once, a boy,
he worked with men
and knew no toy.
Now grizzled and thin,
folds of skin hanging
beneath his chin,
calloused hands clenched,
he lies in bed whimpering:
he has returned to childhood.
Wrapped in bedclothes
he lies staring
at the ceiling.
I feel what he is feeling.
Leaving, I ran my fingers
through his hair,
helped him to his chair,
promised to come again Sunday.
He smiled,
for a moment seemed gay.
His smile still lingers
before my eyes. Now
tears smut my fingers.

(1967)

Soliloquy: November Eighteenth

Dejection dulled your face
as he smirked about babysitting at Welch's.
You didn't look at me:
you sat weakly holding
a spoonful of mint chocolate
ice cream (a small serving)
lost behind deeply veiled blue eyes.

Watching your reaction
I, too, was lost:
what could I say?
what could I do?
We left
not speaking
drifting apart
as the echo of his words
followed us through the damp air,
between the dull-gray parked cars
glimmering in darkness
in the white-lined lot.

Where are we going?
                    I'm taking you home.

Driving through the rain-wet streets
strewn with leaves
I watched your hands,
your brown-spattered blond hair,
as you tried to hide your eyes.

Stopping, we shared
something, I remember,
something that passed

unsure and tentative,
in the rain.

Your tears might have meant more
than the thing you wept for.

(1967)

The Garage

Two rent-a-cars,
one red one white,
stand in the shadow
of the garage
cast by streetlamps
and the flashing
red, white and blue
ESSO sign;
their windows are coated
with a thick layer of ice;
their tires
held fast by drifts of snow.

Four gasoline pumps
stand beneath
a flickering fluorescent lamp.
Their snakelike hoses
bent double
beneath the weight
of driving snow.

A man
stands by the pumps,
hunched over the back
of a car
pumping gas.
Exhaust rises
toward his taut cold face.

I stand in my dark room
by the ice-coated window
twisting my hand in the curtain.
I search for stars
but settle for flashing lights

and the falling snow,
try to understand all these stories
right where they begin.

(1967)

McVey's Barn

McVey's Barn
in the Art Museum,
haunting and dark
with it straw-filled interior
and "Santa's Sleigh"
high on the rotting brown rafters
frightened me:
perhaps it was your attraction to it,
perhaps I feared its beckoning call
and the extended
invisible tendrils
of the rootless straw
grasping me,
pulling me into the dusty bins.

Later,
outside in the snow,
your hand grasped tightly
in mine,
I felt safe.

(1967)

Her Drawing

In a flower-bordered painted field,
among small green shaded hills,
stands a wrinkled tree,
boughs extended.
Legs dangling,
hands grasping
the ropes of a tree swing
suspended from the longest branch,
a small
long blond haired girl sits
watching a plane
in the distance
alone.

Later,
the swing is gone,
the tree has fallen,
the penciled flowers
have withered.

(1967)

Yellow

Stop car. Stop. Car.
Stop.
Alone. Home. Dark.

Wind. Warm.

Yellow.

Hand. You. Smooth.
Fingers. Warm. Gold.

Talk. Kiss. Lips.
Tongue.

I don't want to go....

People. Bus. Boys. Three.
Bicycles. Here. House. You.
Me.
Love.

Yellow.

I have to go.

Kiss. Warm. Hands. Cold.
Ivory.
Touch.
Soft. Hot.
Skin.
Breast. Thigh.
Wet. Wet.
Eyes. Open.

I want to come....

Yellow.

Lips. Tongue. Hair.

Yellow.

I want you.

Yellow.

(1967)

Listen

Wait.

If you stand
in the wind
you may hear
the dark singing of the hills,
the storm's wild words,
the breathless whispers of the stars.

Stop.

Can you hear me?

Listen.

(1967)

an exercise in rhyme

tamed
you saw nothing
and forgave
all

you were
a tailless
alligator
afloat

in the muddied
waters of
a castle's
moat

restless
you were
gone by
fall

(1967)

daisies, lilacs, violets, and dandelions

daisies

white
and yel-
low flow-

ers
on the
hilltop

lilacs

pur-
ple trees
by the

char-
coal drive-
way here

violets

blue-
speckled
grass by

the
water
fountain

dandelions

com-
mon weed
with yel-

low
flowers
growling

(1967)

Thoughts In a Dry Season

Paper thin trees
swaying in the brisk New England breeze
line the freshly tarred street.

Sand left by road crews
crunches beneath my feet
as I make my way to the park.

A dappled gray pigeon
lifts from something half-eaten
by the roadside.

The white streaked sky
is dark and austere, the park's soil
changing to stone.

I finger a blade of grass.
The sun lies atop an old
telephone pole

splintered by the outlines
of black wires
and low clouds.

I leave it dangling
between two cross poles, like
line drawings above the street.

I kick an old baseball bat
lying in the dark grass
by the softball diamond,

its cracked narrow end
hidden by a discarded
yellow ice cream wrapper.

The earth is black and cool.
A dark car stops
with a screech at the corner.

A bird lands in slow motion
on brittle legs, an arc of light
heavy in the trees.

I don't want to die at all.

(1967)

Birdsong

A small red-breasted bird
perched on the outside ledge
of the kitchen window this morning.
Its wings were dripping with rain
and its bill, caked with mud,
held a worm. The window blinds,
half-drawn, dimmed the room,
the walls full of memories,
shadows dry in the far corners.

As it crouched there just before
flight, a drop of water from
the still-leaky storm gutter
hit its back, smoothed
its feathers, left a dark stain.
The bird dropped the worm
and spreading its wings flew past
an abandoned nest high
in the branches of the bare maple.

I could not call it back
and it would not come even
if I knew how to call it,
and I understood then
that our dark shared songs
would fill my dreams,
that I too could find an escape
from all the truths of this house
into a beckoning light.

(1967)

A Very Good Day

The burbling brook flowed on
Unknowing, unsuspecting.
Trees tops swayed
To an unheard melody.
The billowing clouds
Passed by unconcerned.
It was a very good day.

The quiet was broken
By the scream of an eagle
Winging its way towards home.
An eagle with talons of steel.
An eagle unable to feel
The pain and the grief
It would leave on that fateful day.

The eagle came closer.
The good people wailed:
"O Lord forgive us, where have we failed?"
The eagle came closer:
"Kneel down! Let's pray!"
It was the very last day.

The burbling brook flowed on
Unknowing, unsuspecting.
Trees tops swayed
To an unheard melody.
The billowing clouds
Passed by unconcerned.
It was a very *good* day.

(1966)

Golgotha

The hands
Twitched,
Contorted,
Quivered.
Fingers clawing,
Taut hands
Grasping the air,
Pulled fruitlessly.
Clenched fists,
Bare white knuckles,
Slapped
The ageless wood.
Pale skin cracked,
Bled.
Fingers,
Swelled
By splintered wood,
Trembled.
The crucified hands convulsed,
Reached to break bread,
Bless the crowd,
Forgive me
One last time.

(1966)

August 20th

Sitting by the half-opened window,
Looking into the still darkness,
Breathing the rich humid air,
I'm falling asleep.
A faint breeze
Rustles the transparent curtains.

The deathlike stillness
Is shattered by the growl
Of a passing car.
Its red tail lights,
Piercing the shadows of the street,
Glare like the veiled eyes
Of an invisible dragon.
Exhaust smashing into the road
Is smoke from some unearthly fire.
I can't breathe!
Its tin horn bellows its sovereignty,
Warning all
As it lurches along the road.

The car,
Now only a faint reddish glow
In the distance,
Seems unreal
As it sputters down the street.
All that remains
Is the contented chirping of crickets,
Not prone to any mechanical death,
And the rustle of leaves
As summer's thick air rushes past.

(1966)

Through the Looking-Glass

The image stares back.
The face
Is slim and angular.
Deep-set
Small blue eyes
Are liquid in
The harsh light.
Ears are attentive
To the sounds
Of passing cars
In the street,
Scraping chairs
In the room below.
The nose wrinkles:
A sneeze.
The mirror becomes
An ethereal image
Shimmering in kaleidoscope light.
The face, a clown's face,
Is a blotch of reds and whites.
The sounds of crickets chirping
Is a calliope in the distance,
Lights ferris wheels
Turning madly
In some undiscovered carnival.
The sound of passing cars
Is the roar of the crowd,
Scraping chairs
Trumpets in the band.
Peanuts! Popcorn!
Hotdogs!.... Get your hotdogs!...
May I direct your attention
To the center ring here!...
Blinking back the tears

The image suddenly fades,
Leaving nothing but the bare glass
And the clown standing alone
On a sawdust floor,
Arms spread wide
Welcoming the night.
The room is unexpectedly cold,
The walls are smoky and dull,
Each a slightly different color,
No two alike.

(1966)

Note on the Author

Jonas Zdanys, a bilingual poet and translator, is the author of fifty other books, forty-six of them collections of poetry, written in English or in Lithuanian, and volumes of translations of Lithuanian poetry and fiction into English. His most recent book is *Collected Poems 1970–2020*. He serves currently as Professor of English and Poet-in-Residence at Sacred Heart University.

www.ingramcontent.com/pod-product-compliance
Lightning Source LLC
Chambersburg PA
CBHW071320080526
44587CB00018B/3289